PARABLES FROM COMBAT

PARABLES

FROM

COMBAT

SCRIPTURES THROUGH
THE EYES OF A COMBAT VETERAN

Tony Funtanilla

1st Squad, 3rd Platoon, Charlie Company
198th Infantry Brigade, Americal Division
Vietnam 1967-1968

PARABLES FROM COMBAT
Copyright © 2022 Tano Anthony Funtanilla

ISBN 978-1-955008-12-9 paperback
Library of Congress Control Number: 2022912428

Editing by Joyce Magnin
Cover design by Helen Ounjian

Published by Carpenter's Son Publishing
www.carpenterssonpublishing.com

ISBN 978-1-955008-12-9

Printed in the United States of America

This book is dedicated to all of my brothers

who served with me in the

3rd Platoon of Charlie Company,

198th Light Infantry Brigade,

Americal Division in Viet Nam

during 1967 – 1968.

It was such an honor to share the field of battle with some of the most fierce, selflessly reliable, and incredibly brave soldiers to ever serve and fight alongside.

I'd like to give special recognition to Gary Amberson, currently residing in Idaho, and Jim Stringham who lives in Illinois. Back in the day, we fought together, covered each other, laughed and even cried with each other. And now, fifty-four years later, I am extremely blessed to still have them as my most cherished friends. We stay in touch weekly by phone or text and reunite annually in person to share our lives' adventures, boast about our families, joke about our aches and pains, and occasionally talk each other back down from nightmares or flashbacks when they rear their ugly heads. They are two of the finest gentlemen I enjoy the honor of having in my life.

CONTENTS

FOREWORD

In 1966, I was inducted into the U. S. Army and was stationed at Fort Lewis, Washington, for Basic Training. Two years later, I was honorably discharged in 1968 and processed out of the Army at Fort Lewis. Ironically, the same barber who gave me my first military haircut in Basic Training was the same person who gave me my last military haircut two years later when I was discharged from active duty. I knew this because I recognized the tattoo of an eagle on his forearm. After telling him how I recognized who he was, he chuckled and asked how I'd like him to cut my hair. I laughed and told him that I'm not falling for that question again because the first time he cut my hair, I ended up with a complete buzz cut that left me looking like I had undergone chemotherapy. He gave me a big smile and promised not to do that again because the haircut would not be free this time.

Some of what I experienced between my first and last military haircut will be included in this book—not as a typical "war story" documentary, but how I've begun to realize that these experiences are relevant to Christian life and spiritual warfare. I wanted to tell about some of my military experiences and how they've helped me to understand the relevance of Scripture verses more clearly without taking them out of context. In some cases, I chose not to use actual full names out of respect for the families of those who might somehow end up reading this book. My hope is that God will use these parables to help someone else to relate to the Scriptures more vividly as well.

After returning home from the war in Vietnam, like many other combat veterans, I've struggled for years with flashbacks, nightmares, hypervigilance, and all of the typical frustrations associated with PTSD. After giving my life to Christ in 1984, I frequently would pray and even plead for God to take these terrifying memories away from me, but I continue to be haunted by them sometimes to this day. God has always been with me through my struggles, but I've questioned why He still allows them to remain.

Since surrendering my life to Christ in 1984, through hearing numerous church messages, participating in Bible studies, and reading the Word of God, finally now in 2021, I've come to the realization that perhaps God allowed those haunting memories I had buried deep and welded shut to remain because He always has a purpose and a plan for our good. I am convinced in my spirit that part of that plan may well be for my writing the content of this book. I am reminded of the line in the Christian song "See a Victory" that says, "You take what the enemy meant for evil and You turn it for good." My hope and prayer is that this little labor of love will help, inspire, enlighten, or even bring peace to someone who happens to read it. Even if God uses it to affect just one person's spiritual walk, then I consider all of my experiences from the war "have not come back void."

ACKNOWLEDGEMENTS

We all will leave some kind of legacy—good, bad, small, or great—when we leave this world. I wish to thank several people for their unending support, prayers, and encouragement in putting these parables to paper. Numerous pastors faithfully followed the leading of the Holy Spirit by delivering messages and teachings that have greatly affected my walk with God. However, I credit three specific people for being the most influential through their continual encouragement to share my revelations with the rest of the world in this book: my sister-in-law Kathy, who consistently models what it means to tenaciously love, follow, and share all of the biblical teachings of the Lord, and my granddaughter's husband, Josh, who helped me realize that we all have unique God-given insights and artistic abilities that may not suit everyone's taste, but nonetheless they have the potential to touch at least one other person's interest or need. Most gratefully, I thank God for blessing me with my wife, Debbie, who suffered with me, listened to me, supported me, and prayed for me through my remembrances of every flashback and nightmare, and lovingly helped me to realize that I am not the horrible monster that my past tried to convince me I was.

BRONZE
STAR

Parable 1

"His master said to him, 'Well done, good and faithful servant. You have been faithful and trustworthy over a little, I will put you in charge of many things; share in the joy of your master.'"

Matthew 25:21 AMP

At the tender age of nineteen, in Vietnam, I was promoted to the rank of Sergeant E-5 and given the position of 1st Squad leader, which meant I was in charge of a squad of six to eight other soldiers' lives and performance in my platoon. For my duty as a squad leader I was awarded the Bronze Star during my tour in Vietnam, but for years I was not proud about it because it was for "meritorious service," not for any particular act of valor. Although a few events occurred when I acted with total disregard for my own safety to save the lives of fellow soldiers in my charge, they were never witnessed by an officer, which was a requirement for the medal. Officers weren't present either because they were either killed, wounded, or "conveniently" not in close enough proximity to observe those occasions.

Recently though, I realized that "meritorious service" meant that I was recognized for completing every assignment and mission with successful results, often obtaining intel that proved vital to the success of company and brigade-level operations and with minimal casualties. God has given me the revelation that it is far better to be congratulated for a complete tour of exemplary service rather than just one or two acts of valor. Likewise, I would rather have my Lord welcome me into heaven's glory for a life well lived in service to Him, rather than just one or two times when I may have had a positive impact on His kingdom.

NINETEEN YEARS IN THE DESERT

Parable 2

"For those who exalt themselves will be humbled,
and those who humble themselves will be exalted."

Matthew 23:12 NIV

But he gives more grace. Therefore it says,
"God opposes the proud but gives grace to the humble."

James 4:6 ESV

The Spirit you received does not make you slaves, so that you live
in fear again; rather, the Spirit you received brought about your
adoption to sonship. And by him we cry, "Abba Father."

Romans 8:15 NIV

After exiting the Army in 1968, I stopped going to church and acknowledging God. It wasn't that I stopped believing He existed; instead, I just found it difficult to believe he was a fair or just God. I couldn't understand why He would allow some guys who acted like complete low-life idiots who never made any positive contributions to humanity to survive, yet guys whom I viewed as being of the best and most impeccable character often suffered horribly before dying. I've since understood that the devil's mission is to discredit God through unpleasant circumstances. He can only do it in our minds, however, and not in the deepest depths of our hearts.

In the early eighties, I was a fairly successful "lounge lizard" in several local restaurants and bars. After closing for the evening, the staff and I would often hang out around the bar and party. My wife started attending an Assembly of God church and kept trying to encourage me to join her, but because of my mistrust in God, I refused her invitations. She was relentless in trying to convince me that this church was different because of how they promoted the love, peace, and the grace of God. Eventually, I conceded to her persistence and agreed to try it just once. I sat there one Sunday with my arms crossed, and my mind made up to just endure this foolishness, but when the worship music started, tears welled up from my eyes, and I felt strangely broken inside. I convinced myself that it was probably happening because I had partied a little excessively with the restaurant staff the night before, so my nervous system was pretty shaky from being hung over.

During the rest of the week, I pondered what had happened and decided to try attending the church one more time without drinking the previous night. Darn it, to my confusion, the same thing happened again, and then again the following Sunday. Puzzled with curiosity, I continued to attend and started paying attention to what was taught. Eventually, my Jericho walls fell, and I invited Jesus into my heart.

I began to really enjoy going to church for the first time in my life, and since I played guitar and sang as a "former" lounge lizard, I decided that I should join the worship band. However, every time I opened my mouth, I would get so broken and choked up that I couldn't sing. I would get frustrated because I wanted everyone to know how well I believed that I really could sing. I became so frustrated that eventually, I gave up singing and playing the guitar altogether.

My desert from playing guitar and singing came to an end nineteen years later due to the persistence of a friend who was the worship leader at a new church that I attended. He had heard that I once was a musician, so he kept bugging me to pick it up again. Finally, I reluctantly explained to him how my shame for always crying so easily was why I gave up singing and playing the guitar. He graciously helped me to understand how precious and right it was to be so deeply moved whenever connecting to God.

He challenged me to look around and observe what the other men, especially the leaders, were doing during the next worship service. To my great amazement and relief, I saw that they were frequently but unashamedly wiping tears from their eyes. I began to understand what a blessing it truly is to be able to experience such intimacy with my Lord. Once again, I picked up the guitar and opened my mouth to sing His praises, unconcerned about how I sounded to anyone else but my Abba.

EVERY NOTE OF WORSHIP IS LIKE A BULLET SHOT AT SATAN

Parable 3

*When you go to war against your enemies and see horses
and chariots and an army greater than yours,
do not be afraid of them, because the Lord your God,
who brought you up out of Egypt, will be with you.*

Deuteronomy 20:1 NIV

*For the Lord your God is the one who goes with you to fight for you
against your enemies to give you victory.*

Deuteronomy 20:4 NIV

*Have I not commanded you? Be strong and courageous.
Do not be afraid; do not be discouraged,
for the Lord your God will be with you wherever you go.*

Joshua 1:9 NIV

*When I am afraid, I put my trust in you.
In God, whose word I praise —
in God I trust and am not afraid.
What can mere mortals do to me?*

Psalm 56:3-4 NIV

*The Lord is with me; I will not be afraid.
What can mere mortals do to me?*

Psalm 118:6 NIV

*Trust in the Lord with all your heart
and lean not on your own understanding.*

Proverbs 3:5 NIV

I've often wrestled with the concept of the Levites leading the Israelites into battle in the Old Testament. Why have worshiping musicians blowing trumpets and worshiping out loud in front of the Army instead of using the best and heavily armed warriors? Then God put this question in my heart. Knowing what I now know about God and His power, protection, and unending faithfulness, would I prefer to go into battle walking point with my M-16 without Him or with just my guitar and singing His praises with Him by my side?

RELENTLESS

Parable 4

Pray without ceasing.

1 Thessalonians 5:17 KJV

Rejoice in hope, endure in suffering, persist in prayer.

Romans 12:12 NET

And pray in the Spirit on all occasions with all kinds of prayers and requests. With this in mind, be alert and always keep on praying for all the Lord's people.

Ephesians 6:18 NIV

I used to believe that our prayers can change God's mind, but I have also heard that God's will is sovereign and perfect. If that is true and He never makes mistakes, how can our prayers and petitions change His mind? Then I recently heard a teaching that made me rethink my beliefs. The message said that our prayers don't change God's mind, but rather perseverance in our prayers puts pressure on the evil forces that are trying to prevent God's will for our good from coming to fruition. My words aren't active or effective—only God's Word is. We should pray referencing God's WORD continually and without ceasing until the Evil One's attempts to prevent the will of God are extinguished. Please don't think that I'm claiming this is absolutely true. I'm only pointing out that this epiphany reminds me to pray relentlessly.

I'm reminded of the term "suppressive fire" in combat. In other words, in a firefight, you don't just shoot one or two rounds at the enemy and then hope and wait for him to disappear or give up, because he won't. Instead, you keep firing with overwhelming force and, if necessary, call for artillery or air support until the threat is defeated. After the threat is successfully overcome, you stay alert and continue to search for evidence to confirm that the enemy is no longer a threat.

This is also the case when firefighters are trying to contain a raging wildfire. They don't just pour water on the flames once and then wait for the fire to burn itself out. Instead, they continue pouring water on the flames, along with using air-water drops and spraying fire retardant to keep the flames from spreading. Even after the blaze is contained, they still search for and extinguish hot spots in order to ensure no re-ignition of the fire will occur.

WHATEVER
WORKS

Parable 5

For our struggle is not against flesh and blood, but against the rulers, against the authorities, against the powers of this dark world and against the spiritual forces of evil in the heavenly realms.

Ephesians 6:12 NIV

One night while out in the bush, we were dug in for the night. With two to three men in a foxhole, we had to take turns guarding our position while the others slept. This would require us to stay awake and vigilant for one or more hours per shift. Staying awake and alert by yourself was not only scary but very difficult, especially when you're exhausted from firefights or patrolling all day.

Having grown up Catholic, sometimes one activity that helped me stay awake and alert was saying the Rosary. Unfortunately, I never thought to carry a rosary but only the essentials like food, water, hand grenades, and ammo—lots and lots of ammo. Oddly enough, the M-16 has ten vent holes on the top of the foregrip over the barrel, so I realized that my rifle could also double as my Rosary. I would place my finger over the first hole, say a "Hail Mary," then move my finger to the next hole, say another "Hail Mary," and so on until I completed a set of ten. The front sight of my weapon then served as the marker to say an "Our Father," and then I would start all over again. I'm not sure if the pope would have approved of using a weapon as my Rosary, but now as a born-again believer, I feel that it is extremely appropriate. Just like Habakkuk, Job, King David, and numerous others in the Bible who found their strength and courage in the Lord, I gained a sense of security as well.

TREMORS

Parable 6

He said: *"The Lord is my rock, my fortress and my deliverer;*
my God is my rock, in whom I take refuge,
my shield and the horn of my salvation.
He is my stronghold, my refuge and my savior —
from violent people you save me."

2 Samuel 22:2-3 NIV

He says, "Be still, and know that I am God"

Psalm 46:10a NIV

Some may find it counter-therapeutic, but I love watching war movies. They are entertaining to me because I love picking out technical and tactical errors that are committed in them. One of my pet peeves is the way the soldiers in the movies would talk loudly and make excessive amounts of noise while moving through suspected enemy territory. In actual combat situations, visual and especially audio camouflage is crucial to remaining undetected by your adversary. I'm reminded of the movie Tremors, starring Kevin Bacon, in which people are stranded in a desert while being hunted by giant flesh-eating, wormlike creatures that burrow through the sand looking for prey. The characters in the movie eventually discover that these creatures, though equipped with acute hearing, cannot find them if they stand on large boulders and remain very silent.

CHRISTMAS
1967

Parable 7

*For God is not a God of disorder but of peace — as in all the
congregations of the Lord's people.*

1 Corinthians 14:33 NIV

*Dear children, let us not love with words or speech
but with actions and in truth.*

1 John 3:18 NIV

*But someone will say, "You have faith; I have deeds." Show me
your faith without deeds, and I will show you my faith by my deeds.*

James 2:18 NIV

D uring Christmas 1967, our platoon caught a break from being in the bush and was tasked with guarding the Binh San Bridge. We camped under the north end of the bridge, which we fortified with sandbag fighting positions. During the day, we would send out a squad of men to patrol, looking for any evidence of enemy activity near our position. On one such patrol, we passed by a small three-foot-tall tree that resembled a pine tree. Because Christmas Day was approaching, we decided to cut down that scrawny tree and bring it back to our position under the bridge to set up as our Christmas tree. On the way back, we were soon followed by a group of giggling, chattering Vietnamese kids who were puzzled by our excitement over the tree. Back at the bridge, we propped the tree up with sandbags, hung C-Ration can lids with pipe cleaners on it for ornaments, and sprayed shaving cream on it for snow. We also hung Christmas cards from home on it as a finishing touch. This really drove the little kids nuts trying to figure out the reason for all this foolishness.

We found it next to impossible to explain what snow was to someone who had never experienced a climate cold enough to produce it. Worse yet was trying to explain the fat, bearded man in a red suit, flying through the air in a sleigh, pulled by skinny water buffalo-like creatures, with funny horns, and ones with a red nose that were depicted on some of our Christmas cards hanging on the tree.

Possibly the only way they could ever truly understand was by somehow coming to the United States and experiencing this festivity in person. Just like trying to witness to someone about Christianity, this is often best done, not by our words, but by how we live our lives.

PRECIOUS LITTLE CHILDREN

Parable 8

Jesus said, "Let the little children come to me, and do not hinder them, for the kingdom of heaven belongs to such as these."

Matthew 19:14 NIV

During our time under the Binh San Bridge, two little kids always hung around us. Gup was a sweet little girl around eight years old, and her brother, whom we nicknamed "Sluggo," was around six years old. Sluggo, a stocky little guy with not much of a neck, looked like a miniature bouncer. He loved to play-box with us, thus the name Sluggo. Of all the kids from that small village of Binh San, these two were our favorites. They seemed to think everything about us was fascinating: our ways of joking around, our pictures from home, even our sloppy attempt at speaking Vietnamese. Though they had a meager existence, they always had a giggly joy about them, along with a hunger to learn as much as possible about us and the impossible-sounding culture from which we came. Whenever possible, we'd give them food, money, or fatherly wisdom.

Even at the tender age of eight, Gup was very much the big sister to Sluggo. She was almost mothering by the way she would make him behave or straighten up his messy clothes and wipe clean his dusty tears or muddy feet. Eventually, our short time under the bridge ended as duty called. Our higher-ups decided that the area around Binh San was secure enough for us to move on.

We spent the next month or so flushing out suspected Viet Cong activity in other areas. Just before the onset of the 1968

Tet Offensive, we convoyed back through Binh San on our way toward the area outside of Da Nang to check out intelligence reports of an NVA build-up around a hamlet called Lo Giang. While taking a brief rest stop in Binh San, we took that opportunity to go looking for Gup and Sluggo. Tragically, we found out that they were both executed by the Viet Cong to serve as a message to the rest of the villagers of the consequence for fraternizing with Americans. Words could never express the sickening anguish we felt at the thought that their deaths were our fault, nor the animalistic, vengeful hatred we developed toward the Viet Cong.

This account may not appear to have exact relevance to Matthew 19:14, but that verse reminded me of how precious those kids were to us and how much more precious little children are to our God, even to the point of heartbreak when evil and tragedy strikes.

HEROES ARE UNINTENTIONAL

Parable 9

"Greater love has no one than this:
to lay down one's life for one's friends."

John 15:13 NIV

"For my thoughts are not your thoughts,
neither are your ways my ways," declares the Lord.
"As the heavens are higher than the earth,
so are my ways higher than your ways
and my thoughts than your thoughts."

Isaiah 55:8-9 NIV

At the beginning of the 1968 Tet Offensive, Charlie Company was on a mission to investigate a suspected NVA (North Vietnamese Army) build-up near the hamlet of Lo Giang. The NVA were regular Army units from North Vietnam. These enemy soldiers were highly trained, well-equipped, seasoned combat veterans. The 3rd Platoon of Company C led the way across a rice paddy toward a densely wooded area on the far side of the open paddy. On this particular day, my squad was in the lead position.

I ordered "Tank" to walk point, and twenty yards behind him was me, followed by the rest of our platoon. About two-thirds of the way across, all hell broke loose as the NVA opened fire from the tree line. Immediately, I ducked for cover behind a rice paddy dike in front of me while a barrage of bullets zinged over my head and splashed all around my position. Soon after that, I heard the frantic voice of Tank screaming my name, begging for help, and yelling, "I'm hit, I'm hit" over and over. In desperation, I peeked over the dike and saw his hand covered with blood poking up out of the dense reeds of rice. Over and over, he kept calling my name, and all I could think was, "He needs me." There were no "Audie Murphy" thoughts of heroism in my head. All I knew was that my man, my buddy, my brother could be dying, and I was the only person who could possibly do anything about it.

As I lay there, I immediately decided that I would count to three, jump up, and start firing my weapon towards the tree line, and run as low and as fast as I could to get to him. I counted 1-2-3, jumped up, fired one shot, and only heard "click". Tried to fire another round but again "click". Pulled the trigger again only to hear "click" but no "bang", realizing my weapon was jammed. I immediately ducked back down and lay as flat on my back as possible while frantically grabbing for my cleaning rod to unjam the empty shell casing that I realized was stuck in the chamber from my initial shot. All the while, the sound of bullets snapped over me as Tank continued screaming my name. Once my weapon was cleared (no three-count this time), I just jumped up and started running forward, screaming while spraying the tree line with bullets. When I got to him, I discovered that his hip was shattered from an AK47 round, and he was bleeding profusely. Tank continued writhing and screaming in excruciating pain.

From behind me, I heard Jimmy, one of the members of my squad, yelling my name, asking if I was hit. I yelled back that I was okay and to stay away until the shooting subsided, but he ignored my warning and ran to my position, plopping down on top of me. I scooted to my left, out from under him, and told him to keep his head down. Again, he ignored my warning and slowly lifted his head up to look over the rice paddy dike to see where the gunfire was coming from. Just then I heard a sickening smack. Jimmy turned his face toward me, his eyes glazed, and he grunted, "T, my mouth." Then he lowered his head onto my right arm and died with empty eyes still looking at me as blood drained out of his mouth. It turned out that he took a round through his open mouth that lodged in his cervical column.

Shortly after that, our medic, "Doc," miraculously reached us through all the rain of bullets and started treating Tank's injury. It took two or three doses of morphine to get Tank to stop screaming. Meanwhile, bullets kept snapping and zinging over our heads from the tree line in front of us and my fellow soldiers behind us who didn't know we were in front of them.

Things went from bad to worse as we saw one of our gunship helicopters diving toward our open position in the rice paddy. Evidently, our platoon lieutenant was unable to inform the gunship of my location because he was hiding behind cover, calling for airstrikes, and not looking to see where they were hitting. My worst fear came true when the gunship started firing rockets and machine guns at my position. Deafening explosions were going off all around us, causing rice paddy water and huge clumps of mud to rain down on us. We tried our best to use Jimmy's body for a shield. Miraculously, somehow the three of us survived that strafing but noticed the gunship turning to make another run at our position. In a panic, the only thing we could think to do was to open a large field bandage and use Tank's blood to smear a big red cross on it. Laying on our backs as flat as possible, we held the opened bandage over us. Thankfully, as the gunship turned on final approach at us, he noticed our signal and pulled off. We were eventually able to get Tank out safely and "medevaced" to a hospital.

The rest of that day's long battle is a blur to me, probably because I've chosen to not let the memory of it surface yet. In retrospect, I now realize that had I been in my original position before Jimmy plopped down on top of me, I might have been the one shot through the mouth.

I don't understand why God sacrificed Jimmy to save me. All I now know and have to accept is that His thoughts and ways are much, much higher than mine, and He has a purpose and plan for my life.

WHEN THE MACHINE BREAKS DOWN, WE BREAK DOWN

Parable 10

"If a kingdom is divided against itself, that kingdom cannot stand. If a house is divided against itself, that house cannot stand."

Mark 3:24-25 NIV

Then Jesus said to his disciples, "Whoever wants to be my disciple must deny themselves and take up their cross and follow me. For whoever wants to save their life will lose it, but whoever loses their life for me will find it."

Matthew 16:24-25 NIV

People often wonder why drill sergeants are so tough on new recruits during Basic Training. The simple answer is that to become an effective soldier, you must get used to not having your way. In order to cause you to obey orders without question or hesitation, you must lose your civilian attitude of self-indulgence. Orders are given not for your own individual good but for the good of the Army's objectives, which are ultimately to protect and preserve the peace and freedom of your country. You must accept that you are now a part of a fighting machine and will be needed to do things that might get you killed or wounded. In a scene during the movie Platoon, Tom Berenger's character tries to make his men understand how critical it is to not question but obey orders by saying, "When you don't obey what you are told to do, the machine breaks down, and when the machine breaks down, we break down."

IT AIN'T OVER TILL IT'S OVER

Parable 11

But we do not belong to those who shrink back and are destroyed, but to those who have faith and are saved.

Hebrews 10:39 NIV

Be alert and of sober mind. Your enemy the devil prowls around like a roaring lion looking for someone to devour.

1 Peter 5:8 NIV

Be on your guard; stand firm in the faith; be courageous; be strong.

1 Corinthians 16:13 NIV

P rior to being released into actual combat, we were taught that the best defense is an overwhelming aggressive offense known as "firepower." During our first few firefights, the Viet Cong would employ one or two of their soldiers to shoot at us, then run and hide in tunnels or shallow concealment holes called "spider holes." This naturally caused us all to open fire and aggressively pursue them. Once we decided that the engagement was over and had succeeded in shutting down the attack, we would take off our helmets, lay down our weapons, relax, eat, or smoke cigarettes. Knowing this was the habit of GIs, the Cong would then mount a much larger attack on us, catching us completely unprepared to quickly defend ourselves. It didn't take us many more costly scenarios like this to learn that no mater how small or significant the victory, we could never allow ourselves to get too complacent, so we had to always, always, always remain armed and vigilant.

FIRE MISSION!
FIRE MISSION!

Parable 12

Lord, give victory to the king!
Answer us when we call!

Psalm 20:9 NIV

I lift up my eyes to the mountains—
where does my help come from?
My help comes from the Lord,
the Maker of heaven and earth.

Psalm 121:1-2 NIV

"Who of you by worrying can add a single hour to your life?"

Luke 12:25 NIV

He says, "Be still, and know that I am God;
I will be exalted among the nations,
I will be exalted in the earth."

Psalm 46:10 NIV

When firefights begin to intensify, it is crucial to know what resources are available to call upon for support. Depending on your location in proximity to them, you could usually call for additional ground troops, helicopter gunships, close air support jets, artillery, or even B-52 bomb drops. To avoid ineffective use of the support, or worse, "friendly fire" casualties, you must be very concise when trying to communicate via radio the precise location where the fire power would be most effective.

One major problem, however, is that in these times of desperation, your emotions are frantic and your body is dumping uncontrollable amounts of adrenalin throughout your body. This causes your voice to be extremely high-pitched, with your words coming out unclearly at warp speed, all while your thoughts are racing even faster than your mouth can keep up. Thankfully, I was blessed to have a radioman, Specialist 4th Class Godwin, affectionately nicknamed "Screech," who somehow quickly learned to take a deep breath, slow down, and speak clearly when calling in the proper coordinates of how and where to direct the desperately needed support.

AFFECTIONATE NAMES

Parable 13

No longer will you be called Abram; your name will be Abraham,
for I have made you a father of many nations.

Genesis 17:5 NIV

Then the man said, "Your name will no longer be Jacob,
but Israel, because you have struggled with God
and with humans and have overcome."

Genesis 32:28 NIV

When the time came for her to give birth, there were twin boys in her
womb. The first to come out was red, and his whole body was like a
hairy garment; so they named him Esau. After this, his brother came
out, with his hand grasping Esau's heel; so he was named Jacob. Isaac
was sixty years old when Rebekah gave birth to them.

Genesis 25:24-26 NIV

And he brought him to Jesus. Jesus looked at him
and said, "You are Simon son of John.
You will be called Cephas" (which, when translated, is Peter).

John 1:42 NIV

It wasn't uncommon to call each other by just last names or nicknames. For example, one guy's last name was Stringham. It seemed natural to want to call him "String Bean," but since he wasn't at all skinny, we just referred to him as "Bean." Another guy's last name was Ohara. Even though he was Japanese, we simply called him "Irish." Then there was a guy named Tankersly, whom we dubbed "Tank." Gary Amberson was simply "Gare." My best friend was named Benji. Since we were always hanging around together, because he was Japanese and I am Filipino, we were referred to as "Nip and Flip." Almost everyone had some sort of nickname like "Tex," "Weasel," "W3," "Shorty," etc.

After all these years, I am incredibly blessed to still be in constant touch with Bean and Gare. To this day, when we get together and talk about "back in the day," we still refer to everyone else by those nicknames with deeply affectionate and often bittersweet memories. These nicknames will forever connect them to specific significant events in our mind's eye.

UNIFORMS

Parable 14

Therefore, as God's chosen people, holy and dearly loved,
clothe yourselves with compassion, kindness, humility, gentleness
and patience. Bear with each other and forgive one another
if any of you has a grievance against someone.
Forgive as the Lord forgave you. And over all these virtues
put on love, which binds them all together in perfect unity.

Colossians 3:12-14 NIV

A uniform becomes your identity. It helps you recognize who is friendly and who is your foe. It identifies your level of authority. It enables you to become quickly recognized and enhances your ability to stand out in your surroundings. For instance, a policeman's uniform makes his or her purpose obvious. Their badge, rank insignia, weapons, and tactical gear make their authority and ability to enforce it more obvious. However, when they are off duty and in civilian attire, the perception of who they are is not at all apparent. So it is with a soldier. The main difference, though, is that your uniform and all of your gear are designed to not make you easily visible, heard, or become a casualty in combat. The "uniform" of every Christian, on the other hand, should be quite the opposite.

"Nip" and "Flip"
Benji Yamane (KIA 16 March 1968)

UNDER THE Binh San Bridge

"BEAN" "ME" "ROCK"

Christmas 1967

Binh San Bridge

Gup and her Dog
Binh San 1967

"Sluggo"
Binh-San
Dec 1967

Church in Nam

WHOSE VOICE ARE YOU BELIEVING?

Parable 15

"When he has brought all his own sheep outside, he walks on ahead of them, and the sheep follow him because they know his voice and recognize his call. They will never follow a stranger, but will run away from him, because they do not know the voice of strangers."

John 10:4-5 AMP

Nighttime outside the wire was that period when the enemy messed with your mind the most. Sometimes the Viet Cong would throw rocks at different intervals throughout the night, making us think hand grenades were being tossed at us. Whenever we heard a thump in the dark of night, someone would yell, "GRENADE!" making us duck for cover. Not only did ducking for cover make us take our eyes off of the area we were watching over, but yelling "Grenade" helped the enemy to pinpoint our positions. Eventually, we would get so tired of ducking, believing that they were only rocks. But then, BOOM! It was a real grenade!

Sometimes the enemy would often try to mimic the voice of a wounded GI moaning for help in an effort to draw us out from the safety of our foxhole to rescue our comrade. We learned to either challenge their identity with the use of passwords or questions that would only be obvious to an American, like "What state are the San Francisco 49ers from?" Thankfully, their accent and incorrect answers would betray them, and we would immediately light up the night sky with every weapon we had, letting them know that their efforts were foiled. Isn't it great that the Holy Spirit doesn't speak to us with an accent that is difficult to decipher? When we walk in tune with the Holy Spirit, there is no question whose voice is directing our steps.

"CHERRY"

Parable 16

"By their fruit you will recognize them. Do people pick grapes from thornbushes, or figs from thistles?"

Matthew 7:16 NIV

When I was fairly new "in country" (Vietnam), the local kids were always trying to sell us something or offering to do some chore for us to make money. One such child asked me, "Hey GI, shine your shoe? Only one dollar." I didn't really want my boots shined. After all, I would soon be out in the boonies getting them muddy, but thinking that his family needed the money, I said okay. The little guy proceeded to shine my left boot, and when done, he requested his dollar. I said, "Hey, what about my other boot?" to which he smiled and said, "Oh, no problem, GI. Other shoe 5 dollar!" Needless to say, I had to walk around for a while with only one shined boot. Later, after being in country for a while, it was an inside joke that one could spot a "Cherry" (new guy in country) by his one shined boot.

SHORT-TIMER'S CALENDAR

Parable 17

Now listen, you who say, "Today or tomorrow we will go to this or that city, spend a year there, carry on business and make money." Why, you do not even know what will happen tomorrow. What is your life? You are a mist that appears for a little while and then vanishes. Instead, you ought to say, "If it is the Lord's will, we will live and do this or that."

James 4:13-15 NIV

In Vietnam, the normal tour of duty was twelve months. One way everyone would track the number of time left before their "ETS" (Expected Termination of Service) was by keeping what was known as a "short-timer's calendar." It was usually a cartoon drawing of a unique character, typically a drawing of some Disney character or a scantily clad female. The character was divided into 365 numbered squares in sequential descending order. The objective was to color in one square every day, beginning with number 365. In this way, one could visually keep track of how many days he had left before his tour was over, and he would be jumping on the "Freedom Bird" and flying back to "the world" (home). My calendar was an outline of an airline jet, my chariot home.

Far too often, when going through the personal belongings of a fallen comrade to send home to their loved ones, I would find their incomplete short-timer's calendar. The most heartbreaking ones only had a few days left to mark off.

BE CAREFUL WHAT YOU WISH FOR

Parable 18

"Tell the people: 'Consecrate yourselves in preparation for tomorrow, when you will eat meat. The Lord heard you when you wailed, "If only we had meat to eat! We were better off in Egypt!" Now the Lord will give you meat, and you will eat it. You will not eat it for just one day, or two days, or five, ten or twenty days, but for a whole month — until it comes out of your nostrils and you loathe it—because you have rejected the Lord, who is among you, and have wailed before him, saying, "Why did we ever leave Egypt?"

Numbers 11:18-20 NIV

In July 1968, the end of my tour was only a couple of months away. By this time, I was becoming very weary, tired of fighting, and fearful of not surviving to my twelfth month. I thought of shooting myself in the foot to get out of the field but couldn't muster the courage. I even raised my hand out from behind cover once during a firefight hoping to get it shot, that "million-dollar wound." In retrospect, thankfully, my advisories were bad shots.

In 'Nam, every Monday, our medic would issue each of us an anti-malaria pill. I came up with the brilliant idea of getting out of the field by secretly disposing of my Monday pills in hopes of catching malaria. A few weeks later, my grand idea succeeded, and before I knew it, I was on a medivac chopper, delirious but conscious enough to know I was heading to the hospital in Chu Lai. I knew my destination because there were KIA and WIA soldiers also loaded on to the chopper with me.

I must have passed out because the next thing I knew was that my fatigues were completely cut off of me, and I was being splashed with ice-cold alcohol while a large fan was blowing on me. I found out later that this was an initial treatment to try to quickly lower my temperature. I was later told that a temperature over 106 could cause brain damage—mine reached 105 degrees. If you take the most splitting headache you've ever had, which feels like your eyeballs are going to explode out of your head, nausea that feels like you're turning inside out every time you heave, and everything that touches you feels painfully ice cold, but you're sweating profusely because you are burning up, multiply it all ten times, and that's what malaria feels like. Once I was coherent enough to have a few slightly foggy thoughts, I realized what an extremely stupid idea it was to want to catch malaria. Although it got me out of the field for a few weeks, I swore I'd never do that ever again, convinced that getting shot might certainly be far less miserable. After recovering a few weeks later, I found myself back on a chopper to rejoin my unit. All that pain and misery was for nothing.

DIALYSIS

Parable 19

How much more, then, will the blood of Christ, who through the
eternal Spirit offered himself unblemished to God,
cleanse our consciences from acts that lead to death,
so that we may serve the living God!

Hebrews 9:14 NIV

But if we walk in the light, as he is in the light,
we have fellowship with one another, and the blood of Jesus,
his Son, purifies us from all sin.
If we claim to be without sin, we deceive ourselves
and the truth is not in us. If we confess our sins,
he is faithful and just and will forgive us our sins and
purify us from all unrighteousness.

1 John 1:7-9 NIV

My unit would sometimes get orders to recon areas where enemy traffic was suspected. Our task was to visually locate these pathways that were difficult to identify from the air because of dense vegetation. Once located, we would notify Headquarters, who would then send out aircraft to "crop dust" the area with Agent Orange, a chemical used to destroy vegetation, thus making these traveling routes used by the enemy more detectable by our observation aircraft. When the crop dusters neared our location, we were told to lie face down on the ground and hold our breath as the herbicide was being sprayed all around and over us. I remember trying to wipe the oily substance off of my arms and neck once the spraying was completed. Years later, it was determined that Agent Orange was highly carcinogenic and responsible for many health-related illnesses. Part of my service-connected health issues like diabetes and gastrointestinal disease are presumed to be related to my exposure to Agent Orange.

My brother, who served in Vietnam before me, also suffered from exposure to Agent Orange. His struggles were diabetes, kidney failure, congestive heart failure, and poor circulation in his lower extremities. Eventually, his kidney failure necessitated that he undergo dialysis treatments three times a week. With dialysis, a tube was inserted into an artery in his arm, which ran his blood into a machine that would cleanse it of toxins the way his kidneys were no longer able to do. Then the clean blood was returned via a different tube into a vein in his arm. The whole process took about four hours to complete.

This treatment reminds me of how Jesus cleanses us of all our worldly toxins and that we must be "plugged" into Him in order to receive that cleansing. Jesus is our spiritual dialysis machine. Thankfully, we only have to say "yes" to His cleansing lordship once instead of three times a week for four hours at a time.

IRRETRIEVABLE

Parable 20

If you return to the Almighty, you will be restored:
If you remove wickedness far from your tent
and assign your nuggets to the dust,
your gold of Ophir to the rocks in the ravines,
then the Almighty will be your gold,
the choicest silver for you.

Job 22:23-25 NIV

One of my favorite passages in the Bible is Job 22:21-30. In verse 24 it talks about assigning your gold to the rocks in the ravines. One day while on a mission, we were traversing a river bed of mostly large boulders. Most were the size of Volkswagens mixed in with various smaller ones. As I was jumping from boulder to boulder, I dropped my favorite Zippo lighter while attempting to light a cigarette. Trying to catch it, all I could do was watch as it bounced from rock to rock and then disappeared down a tight crack between two boulders into the water. My heart sank in frustration, realizing that it would be impossible to retrieve. The lighter was a high school graduation present from my girlfriend with our names in a heart engraved on it. Not only did it have sentimental value, but having something to light the fuse of an explosive or a fire to heat food was an absolute necessity. Losing that lighter has now given me a vivid picture of what it means to get rid of valued worldly things so completely that they are irretrievable.

THERE ARE NO ATHEISTS IN FOXHOLES

Parable 21

So in Christ Jesus you are all children of God through faith, for all of you who were baptized into Christ have clothed yourselves with Christ. There is neither Jew nor Gentile, neither slave nor free, nor is there male and female, for you are all one in Christ Jesus.

Galatians 3:26-28 NIV

"No one has greater love [nor stronger commitment] than to lay down his own life for his friends."

John 15:13 AMP

One who has unreliable friends soon comes to ruin, but there is a friend who sticks closer than a brother.

Proverbs 18:24 NIV

When mayhem begins to explode all around, it's not uncommon to hear someone scream or shout "Oh God!" or "Jesus Christ!" Whether it's an intentional cry for supernatural help or just a knee-jerk reflex expletive, it amazes me what comes out of one's mouth in a moment of extreme fear or desperation. When bullets start to fly, no one cares if you are yellow, black, brown, or white. It makes no difference what political party you support or spiritual beliefs you cling to, not even if you love or detest country, Latin, or Motown music. All that matters most is that the guys next to you can be relied upon to do their part and whatever is required to defeat the enemy and help you stay alive.

We had a saying: "For those of us who have fought for it, life has a meaning the protected will never know." When you eat, sleep, cry, fight with all your might, and share your fears together under extreme circumstances, you are no longer just friends but become closer than brothers. Knowing that we would quickly disregard our own safety to save or protect each other without hesitation and having confidence in mutual reciprocation is the essence of brotherhood.

LEARNING TO SLEEP WITH ONE EAR OPEN

Parable 22

In peace I will lie down and sleep,
for you alone, Lord,
make me dwell in safety.

Psalm 4:8 NIV

I lie down and sleep;
I wake again, because the Lord sustains me.

Psalm 3:5 NIV

In vain you rise early
and stay up late,
toiling for food to eat—
for he grants sleep to those he loves.

Psalm 127:2 NIV

When you lie down, you will not be afraid;
when you lie down, your sleep will be sweet.

Proverbs 3:24 NIV

Those Scriptures are often used to reference that sleep is a gift from God. Anyone who has been a combat soldier knows how precious sleep is. Whether you are out in the bush or back at a base camp or landing zone (LZ), you are always taking turns vigilantly pulling security watch, usually for an hour or more every night. Even when it is your turn to sleep, you have to learn to sleep lightly so that you can be ready to engage the enemy at a moment's notice.

Often when out on a night ambush, we would sleep sitting up back to back with a buddy and our rifles across our laps so that we could immediately wake up with weapons in hand as soon as the ambush was triggered. Sitting upright was also a good way to prevent snoring when noise discipline was paramount. I once had a new replacement in my squad who had a problem staying awake during his turn to pull watch at night out in the boonies. I told our platoon sergeant about this dangerous dilemma, and he told me to have the new soldier come to see him the next time it was his turn to pull guard. The next night, when it was the newbie's turn to pull watch, I told him to go see the platoon sergeant first. Evidently, Sgt. "R" took a hand grenade, pulled out the retaining pin, and told the newbie to hold on to it without letting go of the grenade spoon until his guard time was over. Then, he was instructed to return the grenade to Sgt. "R" so that he could replace the pin to render it safe again, which he did. The poor kid's grip was so tightly locked around the grenade that it had to be pried out of the wide-awake soldier's hand. Obviously, the kid understood that if the rest of us heard an explosion, it would confirm his inability to stay awake, which would earn him a trip home . . . in a body bag. Needless to say, he never fell asleep again during his watch.

Over fifty years later, I've discovered that I'm still somewhat of a light sleeper. I have one of those fitness smartwatches, and it shows that my deep sleep is short and scattered throughout the night. However, my light sleep occupies a higher percentage than what's considered normal. According to Google, this is often indicative of someone who maintains a level of hypervigilance. Fortunately, God has blessed me with the ability to fall asleep quickly and usually stay asleep through the night, unless, of course, I hear an unfamiliar noise during the night. Looking back on all that I've gone through, I now consider that sleep truly is a gift from God.

STEP BY STEP

Parable 23

"Enter through the narrow gate. For wide is the gate and broad
is the road that leads to destruction, and many enter through it.
But small is the gate and narrow the road that leads to life,
and only a few find it."

Matthew 7:13-14 NIV

Whoever strays from the path of prudence
comes to rest in the company of the dead.

Proverbs 21:16 NIV

Let your eyes look directly ahead
And let your gaze be fixed straight in front of you.
Watch the path of your feet,
And all your ways will be established.
Do not turn to the right or to the left;
Turn your foot from evil.

Proverbs 4:25-27 NASB

ecause we GIs hated getting our feet wet, we would walk along the rice paddy dikes whenever we had to traverse the knee-deep flooded paddies in the flatlands. Sometimes the Cong would snipe at us while on the dikes, knowing that our natural reaction was to jump off of the dikes to take cover. The VC would place sharpened bamboo stakes dipped in human feces called "punji sticks" just off the sides of the dikes, hidden just under the water line in anticipation that we would dive off and impale ourselves on the sticks. If getting stabbed by the bamboo didn't take us out of action, the infection from the feces would. They also employed this punji stick tactic along narrow footpaths in the jungles.

After the monsoon season ended, we were sent on a recon mission to the Laotian border. Our task was to confirm suspected activity along the Ho Chi Minh Trail. However, the coordinates we were given to recon put us a few klicks (kilometers) inside Laos. At that time, our so-called political but non-tactical experts decided that Americans should not be allowed in Laos or Cambodia.

An intense firefight broke out when an overwhelming number of the North Vietnamese Regular Army soldiers (NVA) discovered our presence. Outnumbered and unable to get air support because U. S. troops weren't supposed to be in Laos, we had no choice but to pull a hasty retreat and fight our way back across the border before being able to get any sort of support. The enemy knew that we GIs often traveled the same route back. So to avoid running into an ambush, we took a different, more direct route back toward the Vietnam border.

This route took us to a deep gorge with a river running swiftly through it. The only way available to cross was by a narrow wooden footbridge. It was such a narrow bridge that we had to cross in single file, even while trying our best to carry our wounded. Being somewhat acrophobic, I had to really try to focus on not looking down or to either side to avoid getting paralyzed with fear while holding up the others from getting to the other side quickly. It was literally the narrow path that led to life.

BAD DECISION

Parable 24

If someone asks, 'What are these wounds on your body?'
they will answer, 'The wounds I was given
at the house of my friends.'

Zechariah 13:6 NIV

As my tour progressed, I found myself being temporarily on loan to other companies in our brigade because of losses to their leadership ranks. I took over leading squads in Alpha, Bravo, and Delta Companies from time to time to help cover gaps in their platoons while helping to train new replacements. One night when I was finally back with Charlie Company, we were struggling to move quietly through waist-high brush. The evening sky was overcast, making it extremely dark and hard to identify our direction of travel. I recognized the terrain since I had been through there previously while on loan to Alpha Company. I decided to make my way up to our company commander (without using his real name, I'll just refer to him as Captain "B") so that I could inform him that I knew of a trail about fifty yards off to our right that we could use to get out of the noisy brush that we were in. He appreciated my advice and told me to lead the way. I took point, and the rest of the company followed. We carefully made our way to the trail.

Once on the trail, the going became much easier, and thankfully the cloudy night sky began to break up slightly, giving us tiny bits of moonlight to help me see ahead. The brush that lined the sides of the trail started to become taller and taller until it was about head high. The thought occurred to me that this was becoming too ideal an opportunity for us to walk into an ambush, so I signaled for the column behind me to halt.

Instinctively, they got low with their weapons, alternately pointing left and right. Just then, I heard a rustling in the bushes ahead on my right, so I knelt down on one knee, clicked the safety on my rifle off, and raised it to my shoulder. I could barely make out the silhouette of a rifle poking out from the bush. First, an arm and then a body completely emerged into the open. With my heart pounding rapidly in my throat, I quickly rattled off three rounds center mass and then lay down flat in case there was return fire. The body collapsed to the ground, and I waited for what seemed like an eternity until I felt it seemed safe to move forward to check the situation out.

Slowly and quietly, I stepped forward in a crouch until I reached the body. In the dim shadows, I was horrified to discover it was Captain "B." I signaled for the guys behind me to move up to my position. When they joined me, I agonizingly choked out the words, "My God, it's Captain B." Suddenly, a voice frantically cried out, "Don't shoot, don't shoot!!" from inside the bush. I spun around and pointed my weapon toward the sound of the voice and demanded he come out and identify himself. It was "Screech," the captain's radioman, who had been pointing his rifle at my head, ready to fire until he recognized my voice and came out of the bushes. Our medic started administering aid to Captain B and advised Screech to call for a medivac. Miraculously, my shots were slightly low and missed hitting any vital organs. I later found out that two rounds hit his abdomen, and the third hit him in the groin.

Because it was a friendly fire incident, I was ordered to board the medivac chopper with Captain B so that the circumstances of the shooting could be investigated back at base camp headquarters. Prior to being shipped to the hospital at Chi Lai, the captain admitted that he made a bad decision for him and his radioman to continue pushing straight forward through the brush so that they could rendezvous with the rest of us on the trail. For some unknown reason, though, he failed to let the rest of us know.

Thankfully, the investigation determined that the shooting did not happen because of any negligence on my part. Nevertheless, knowing that I was the one responsible for him never being able to father any children, along with experiencing paralysis for the rest of his life, made me never want to shoot a gun ever again. Regardless, after undergoing a psychiatric evaluation, I was ordered to rejoin my unit back out in the field. About a decade later, I heard rumors that he had committed suicide because he refused to live without the use of his legs or manhood due to his own bad decision. Looking back, I have to credit my loving God for covering me with the strength, grace, and mercy to live with the heavy burden of being the one who pulled the trigger that horrible night.

I'M OUT OF HERE!

Parable 25

When his time of service was completed, he returned home.

Luke 1:23 NIV

For while we are in this tent, we groan and are burdened,
because we do not wish to be unclothed
but to be clothed instead with our heavenly dwelling,
so that what is mortal may be swallowed up by life.

2 Corinthians 5:4 NIV

The day finally came when I could mark off the last square on my short-timer's calendar. My platoon lieutenant gave me the thumbs up to gather my gear and get on the last supply chopper heading back to Headquarters in Chu Lai. It was bittersweet saying goodbye to my buddies and wishing them well, with promises to connect with their families back in the world.

I spent that night in our brigade base camp in Chu Lai. After turning in my gear, I boarded a C-130 the next morning for a quick flight to the Americal Division Headquarters in Cam Ranh Bay. There I was able to take a real soap-and-water shower and was issued a fresh set of Class 2 dress khakis. Best of all, I was issued orders authorizing me to leave Vietnam. It felt strange not to be clothed in jungle green. I especially felt naked without my M-16 and bandolier of ammo. Everyday activities that especially fascinated me included experiencing my first reunion with a real flushing toilet and standing under an endless supply of the hot running water of a shower, which I hadn't had the luxury of in a year. In the bush, the longest we ever went without any sort of soap-and-water cleansing was forty-two days. Needless to say, this was a real treat.

The flight home was definitely an unforgettable experience. All of the stories of the dead silence on board the plane with everyone holding their breath until the wheels lifted off of the runway don't even come close to how it really felt. The plane erupted with loud, jubilant shouts of joy, fist bumps, high-fives, hugs, tears, and giving the finger to the fading landscape as we headed out over the South China Sea.

We had a layover in Okinawa that lasted several agonizing hours because of some kind of mechanical issue. This caused us to worry if the fear of dying before getting home would ever end. Thankfully though, we eventually were wheels up back in the air, homeward bound.

Finally, after what seemed like an eternity, we felt the plane bump and heard the most beautiful sound of the landing gear screech as we landed on real U. S. soil. Once more, the plane erupted with shouts of joyous celebration. When we got off the plane, an officer greeted us and ordered us to get in formation and then assume the push-up position on the ground, which we obeyed with defiance. To our delight, he then said, "You may now kiss the ground, men. YOU ARE FINALLY HOME ON AMERICAN SOIL!"

After a short bus ride, we arrived at Fort Lewis, Washington, to begin processing out of the Army and back into civilian life. Just seventy-two hours earlier, I was a heavily armed combat soldier in the jungle. I found it odd to believe I would no longer be in a hostile environment and noticed that the air smelled fresh and clean, not heavy and stale with the scent of rotting vegetation and flesh. I still felt psychologically dirty and hypervigilant, wondering if I would ever remember how to be a human again.

PTSD

Parable 26

Whoever conceals their sins does not prosper,
but the one who confesses and renounces them finds mercy.

Proverbs 28:13 NIV

When you enter the military, you initially spend about ten weeks in Basic Training learning how to be a soldier, then another couple of months in AIT (Advanced Individual Training), honing your designation military occupational skills. In my case, it was the infantry. After arriving in Vietnam, we underwent two more weeks of jungle warfare training, perfecting ways to kill and hopefully not be killed. The end of my military service coincided with the end of my tour in Vietnam.

Because we are immediately released back into society with absolutely no "un-training" whatsoever, it's no wonder that many of us veterans struggle with readjusting to civilian life. Feelings of guilt, remorse, or regret over what we did or didn't do, knowing what we were or should have been, and remembering the things we witnessed or caused are all ingredients for PTSD. I've come to accept that all of the guilt, remorse, and regret have everything to do with the past, but they also have the power to ruin your future if they're left unaddressed and untreated. Sadly, when ignored, too many vets end up homeless, suffer from mental instabilities, self-medicate with drugs and alcohol, experience isolation, or even commit suicide. It is my belief that it is all because of a lack of knowledge about resources, "un-training," and God.

MY FIRST DAY HOME

Parable 27

Trust in the Lord with all your heart
and lean not on your own understanding;
in all your ways submit to him,
and he will make your paths straight.

Proverbs 3:5-6 NIV

"For I know the plans I have for you," declares the Lord, "plans to
prosper you and not to harm you, plans to give you hope and a future.

Jeremiah 29:11 NIV

After this, he will turn back toward the fortresses of his own country
but will stumble and fall, to be seen no more.

Daniel 11:19 NIV

So there I was, finally on an airliner heading to San Francisco. Landing there, I was shocked at my first sight of hippies. No neat hairdos, button-down collars, white Levis, and Converse tennis shoes like before I left. Now I saw people with long, dirty hair, long sideburns with mustaches, pastel-colored sunglasses, and bell-bottom pants. Wow, did I feel out of place being well groomed with shined shoes in my dress green uniform decorated with insignias and ribbons. I walked past one such hippie-looking guy who actually sneered at me, spat, and called me a coward for refusing to go to Vietnam. The pride of wearing a uniform, which indicated that I faithfully served my country, started to fade into puzzling shame.

My parents didn't know that I was on my way home yet. My plan was to hop on the commuter helicopter flight at the San Francisco Airport and fly across the bay to the Oakland Airport, then catch a taxi home to San Leandro about ten miles away and surprise my family. I got my ticket for the helicopter, but fifteen minutes before the scheduled flight, my name was called at the check-in counter. There, I was informed that my seat had been bumped because civilians were given priority seating over military standby personnel. I figured, No problem. I've waited a year to get home; I can wait a little longer. The next available flight would be in thirty minutes, so I complied.

A few minutes before that scheduled flight, the same thing happened again. Again, I was being bumped off for someone else. I tried to explain that I was actually now a civilian, but the uniform I was wearing were the only clothes I had. I even showed the ticket agent my discharge papers and told her that I had been overseas, and all I wanted was to get home and see my family, who had been worried about me for the last twelve months. She apologized and promised to get me on the next flight after the lunch hour. Angrily, I slammed my ticket on the counter and demanded a refund while she muttered something under her breath about me being a crazy, wild animal. Now that my plan had been ruined, I found a payphone and called my parents to tell them where I was so that they could come get me.

Once home, and after all of the excitement and tears of joy subsided, I borrowed my dad's car and drove over to my girlfriend's house at the time, still in my uniform, to see the girl who kept me fighting to survive for all these past twelve long months. Her mother greeted me at the door but awkwardly invited me in. I sat in her living room and was told that my girlfriend was out shopping but should return soon.

Soon my girlfriend's younger brother excitedly bolted into the room, exclaiming, "Hey, guess what? I'm going to be an uncle!" His mother tried to hush him up, and she said, "I'm so very sorry, but she got herself into trouble while you were gone." Not really wanting confirmation, I asked what she meant, and she ashamedly informed me, "It was a big mess, but now she is pregnant." Stunned and bewildered, at a total loss for words, I excused myself and just left. I got in my car dazed, heartbroken, and very angry.

The only thing I wanted to do was head straight for the local recruiting office to reenlist and request to be shipped back to Vietnam, where I believed that at least back there, I had some black-and-white control over my day-to-day existence. Coming to a screeching stop in front of the recruiter's office, I encountered yet another blockade to a happy homecoming experience. The recruiting office was closed because it just happened to be Sunday. I screamed a blistering "WELCOME @#$% HOME @#$%!"

I have since realized how grateful I am to God that He didn't allow me to go back to Vietnam. I had a cousin who had a similar disappointment and volunteered to go back to 'Nam but ended up getting his name on the Vietnam Memorial Wall in Washington, DC. I sincerely thank the Lord that He had other plans and purposes for my life. Looking back, even with life's ups and downs, I can truly say that overall, I've enjoyed an extremely blessed and fruitful life. And again, maybe, just maybe, this book was destined to be part of it.

Charlie 3-1 Over and Out

IN MEMORIAM

3rd Platoon, Charlie Company
198th Light Infantry Brigade,
Americal Division
Viet Nam, 1967 - 1968

SP4 James Stanley Cerione III
KIA 8 February 1968

SP4 Richard Lee Claverie
KIA 4 March 1968

CPL Douglas Lee Harrison
KIA 2 April 1968

SGT Benji Yamane
KIA 16 March 1968

SP4 Steve Masao Ohara
KIA 1 September 1968

123

MEET THE AUTHOR

Tony Funtanilla was born in Oakland, California, where he spent his early childhood. One summer, when he was eight, his parents enrolled him in the local YMCA where he became friends with Benji Yamane, a Japanese boy around his age. They hung out and spent the entire summer swimming and playing pool, but at summer's end, they went their separate ways. Tony and his family moved to San Leandro, California, where he completed his formative school years. After graduating from high school in 1966, he was drafted into the Army a month after his eighteenth birthday.

Being away from home in boot camp at Fort Lewis, Washington, was hard enough, but that feeling faded somewhat when he reconnected with his friend, Benji. They became very close friends, even sharing the same platoon. Later that winter, they were both transferred to Fort Hood, Texas, for Advanced Individual Training (AIT), once again sharing the same platoon. The twosome soon became known as "Nip and Flip," Benji

being Japanese, and Tony, Filipino. By late summer, their unit shipped out to Viet Nam and, as fate would have it, Benji and Tony were once again in the same platoon. Eventually, Benji and Tony were separated by Benji's promotion to Platoon Sergeant and reassigned to Delta Company, while Tony stayed with Charlie Company. Devastatingly, Benji lost his life there.

I often wonder if he'd still be alive had we stayed together, Tony thought, *or perhaps I would have been killed with him since we were always together. In retrospect, God had other plans for my life.* "But oh, how I still miss you, Benji."

After his military time was up, Tony returned to California where he worked, met his wonderful wife, found the Lord Jesus Christ, and enjoyed leading worship. He and Debbie now reside in Texas. They have three daughters who blessed them with nine incredible grandchildren, five granddaughters, and four grandsons who love God and live in California.

Tony's life is a testament to the trials and sadness he has endured, leaving him with the realization he is fully living an extremely blessed life that has come full circle. Happily retired and aware of how the Lord has refined and led him each step of the way, he lives with a strong sense of purpose. Prompted by the Holy Spirit to write this devotional to inspire and uplift others, his hope is that God will impart joy and insight through these pages to you, the reader.

All to the glory of God.

ORDER INFO

For autographed copies or speaking engagements,
contact the author:
Tony Funtanilla
tfuntanilla@gmail.com

Also available from your favorite bookstore
Like us on Facebook

Printed in the USA
CPSIA information can be obtained
at www.ICGtesting.com
JSHW012055140824
68134JS00035B/3446

9 781955 008129